BLOOD WEATHER

poems

BLOOD
WEATHER

Alice Friman

LOUISIANA STATE UNIVERSITY PRESS
BATON ROUGE

Published by Louisiana State University Press
Copyright © 2019 by Alice Friman
All rights reserved
Manufactured in the United States of America
LSU Press Paperback Original

DESIGNER: Michelle A. Neustrom
TYPEFACE: Sina Nova

LIBRARY OF CONGRESS CATALOGING-IN-PUBLICATION DATA

Names: Friman, Alice, author.
Title: Blood weather : poems / Alice Friman.
Description: Baton Rouge : Louisiana State University Press, [2019] |
   Includes bibliographical references.
Identifiers: LCCN 2019007986 | ISBN 978-0-8071-7006-9 (pbk. : alk. paper) |
   ISBN 978-0-8071-7257-5 (pdf) | ISBN 978-0-8071-7258-2 (epub)
Classification: LCC PS3556.R5685 A6 2019 | DDC 811/.54—dc23

*In memory of Roy Marz, who taught me how to love poetry, and
Judith Kitchen, who taught me how to read it*

CONTENTS

BLOOD WEATHER

Drawing the Triangle

Mathematics can be more exquisite than poetry.
—YAKOV SINAI

Outside my window
the hawk reels exquisite,
circling down. Point of view
is all it takes to name a spiral
of death exquisite. To the mouse
running desperate, any hole
under the darkening shadow
would prove the same.
                    But to the hawk
whose chicks wait in the tall pine,
open-beaked and insistent, that mouse—
frozen now and shivering in his velvet,
the beads of his eyes registering
the blank of nowhere to hide—is exquisite.
                    And so geometry
dictates. I watch the hawk, the hawk
the mouse, the mouse (poor thing)
the haven that's not there. It's here.
You're looking at it.

I

Once Upon a Time

I tell about a tour group
traveling in a foreign country,
and of the woman who at a rest stop
went inside to change her clothes.
When she returned to the bus—
Where's the lady in the pink shirt?
So a search party was formed, and she
joined in, searching for herself.

Not metaphorically as those words imply:
Thoreau deep in Walden Woods,
seeing himself in the soarings of a hawk.
But actually, the way, startled, you glimpse
in a passing mirror yourself as stranger:
an old lady wearing hurt on her face
like an abandoned child.

The question is, did she find herself.
Or did someone else suddenly
turn and say, *You're it!*
You, the person everyone's looking for.

Isn't that what we all want?
To be the person everyone's looking for?

Strapped in our seats, the bus stinking
of diesel, heading north, south, anywhere
and, for once, given a chance
to claim a life of shining achievement
just by changing a pink shirt to blue.
Mother Teresa. Madame Curie.
Why, I could be Emily Dickinson

in a white dress, having stuffed my
green sweatshirt with the stained sleeves
in a trash bin sixty miles east of Toledo.

The Interview

You ask who's to blame. Me.
I am to blame. For what?
Maybe the whole business.

You ask where I come from.
If I knew I'd tell you. Could be
I'm still there. But right now

I'm by the river. I go there
looking for four-leaf clovers.
When I find one, I give it away.

If you come, I'll give you
a fresh one for your buttonhole.
What I remember most

about the earth? A pond I saw
late one spring afternoon, algae
inching out from the edges—

a green sludge that by late July
would meet in the middle,
buttoning the pond up for good.

An old sweater. A blind man's
eye. I saw dragonflies too—
jewels flitting over the water

fastened to each other. It seems
nature's way, this buttoning.
And there were creature stirrings

like castanets, and from far away
an elegy of tin flutes. I hope
you will come. I've pressed a few

four-leaf clovers in a book in case
I can't find new ones anymore.
And since you asked, yes, I much

prefer quiet. A hush, a silence.
The marbles of ancient Greece
made vivid speech by gleaming.

White Out

My bedroom window has developed
    an air leak, making this winter day
        glitter on the other side of a fog,

the way a dream holding the secret
    of everything winks from beyond waking
        and will not come clear. Two panes

joined at the frame have achieved
    the impossible: caught a cloud
        that neither dissipates nor floats off

season after season, year after year.
    An immortal wisp: a rag
        of the ineffable garment, captured

mid-flight and saved in perpetuity
    like saints' knuckles in a crystal case.
        But there I go, waxing dramatic again:

a leak in a double-sheet window
    given such significance. You'd think
        I was imitating Melville, who turned

the mountain he looked at from his window
    into a great white whale: the symbolic
        phantom his crazed captain

could not see beyond. And yet,
    out my window, there in the midst
        of a glass clarity—a patch of vapor

like a boomerang flings back at me
    the white wall of my old sorrow
        that I too cannot see beyond.

From the Book of Accounts

I speak of work. How he'd come home
coughing wet and loose in the chest

from the Chesterfields, the hauling
of bundles. How he'd stumble to the sofa—

long underwear drooping at the seat—
flop down, snoring before his head

hit the armrest. Seven o'clock and blotto
as a burnt-out bulb, while across the room

far into the night Mother and I for her sake
played cards, shuffled and dealt, shuffled

and dealt. So much thin-lipped work
it took to arrange and rearrange

the hand she'd been given. So much
work to have to pick up every morning

the death card of hard labor
that any cut deck eventually lays bare.

All those hours of heavy lifting
to gather, dole out, and try again—

draw and discard, draw and discard
amid grunts from the sofa—troubled dreams

and fortune's shuffle. Night after night,
the long march of deuces and kings,

three of a kind, four of a kind, any kind,
before she'd finally get up to shake his shoulder

and walk him to bed, while I'd wait for her
to come back, sit down, and tally up the points.

The Visitation

The white oak outside my window
turns burgundy as befits the season.
But this fall, as if bursting in a boast
of fang and claw, the tree has turned
red, animal red—blood sister
to the circling hawk. No other oak
in the surrounding forest matches it.
No other tree. If this visitation
is a sign to be read through glass—
museum diorama or a crystal ball
that seizes, shrinks, and reports
what's hoped for—I can't say. I only
know the tree presses to my window,
holding out its palms for me to read:
ten thousand hands fluttering murder.

I think Shakespeare, Birnam Wood
come to Dunsinane and all that.
But this time Birnam Wood
has come to me, hoisting in my face
the army's standard, its prized
rallying point: the lady of the house
on a spiked pole bloated by blood.

Soon the leaves will darken the way
all blood darkens when exposed to air.
And drifts of the dull and desiccated
will fall like scabs. Pathetic fallacy,
I know—heaping butchery on a tree.
But my time is short, and I, with no
camera or Crayolas, have only
these lines to lasso this red down:
a necessity come winter when all color

drains out of this world, and I am left
pacing my discontent before my night window
where outside, a skeleton nightgowned in fog
rocks in the cold, periodically
scraping the ground, feeling for her hands.

Lady Macbeth

If you must, fault her for having
abandoned her own life until it echoed
hollow as the crown he tightened
around her head. But who can separate
the tangled coils of mating bodies?
Having no center, she latched on to his,
using the only art she had—the hiss
of influence. And he, like a snake
lapping yolk from an egg, drained her.

Think of the hours she spent
waiting, hanging on each letter,
bathing herself, creaming herself,
for wasn't he her all in all—
the mouth of him, the sweaty
smell of him, the ropey arms she'd
crawl into, cherished as the crown
she thought she was to him, the him
who swore they'd be together, love-
locked even to the slime pits of hell,
the him to whom she gave her everything—
breasts, belly, hands. Oh, how he'd
fondle her hands, feast on her hands,
undress them slowly, slipping off
each ring, licking each knuckle. Who
was she looking for that terrible
sleepwalking night? An empty
wraith sucked dry and used up.
What was left of her
at the end to wash?

Whose blood was that?

Mirage

Across Kachemak Bay
black mountains rise like judgment
towering above the inlet, black
streaked with snow. Black,
white. Nothing in between.

When suddenly like a phantom
floating across the water,
a fishing boat chugs past, and there
we are again, steaming out of Freeport
with Captain Charlie. Little family
bundled up against the cold.

And it must be close to noon
for there's Mother doling out
the egg-salad sandwiches loaded
with lettuce for health and green
good fortune. The bay too, a green
bounty crowned by white flashes
of gulls skimming low over the stern
to eye what the wake churned up.
And look, there at the rail, chumming
for fish, that's my father, roaring
his smutty songs with Mother laughing
because they were in the open air
and free to let themselves be—Oh
dare I say it—happy. What difference
if the fluke or flounder weren't biting,
for wasn't it fluke enough their being
at peace for just this once? On the scales

of judgment, shouldn't that day—snatched
from the angry current of the rest—count?
Add up to something? That day when the gulls
weighed in, balancing the light on their wings.

Asking Forgiveness

for Bruce

When we cleaned out Daisy's house,
dragging one hundred and twenty-six
black bags to the curb. When you
packed up the basement and garage
while I opened her top dresser drawer
to fold—*gently gently*—what no
mere daughter-in-law has rights to.
Then suddenly, because how could
she be gone, I saw her hands again
patting her fresh-from-the-beauty-parlor
hair, the same style as in the photos
taken when she was twenty—photos
found in a shoebox stuffed with letters
from her Robert and the war. Photos
you spread out on all the little tables
at the viewing, passing them among
the guests—*see, see what she was*—
while she, in her travel clothes, lay
among us, oblivious for the first and
only time to the choke of your sorrow.
What could I do to save you, having
myself to beg pardon for? I stood
by her box and, sliding my hand in
to finger the white collar of her dress,
asked forgiveness. For I had taken
in my two rough hands the forbidden
of another: the cotton-crotched, the lace-
trimmed, the cupped, the pink and final
nightgown. The delicates worn and warmed
by her, the crushables that clung to her:
her fragile comforts, her son.

All for the Love of You

On the day Daisy just plain
died, Kenneth Haydon of Benton
"left earth to shake hands with Jesus"
and La'Kesha Walker, youngest
of six, "passed through the gates
of Heaven." Whether angels sang
or if there were hugs, backslapping,
or kisses on both cheeks *à la française,*
I don't know, but I tell you,
it was a great day here on Earth
for the Paradise Casket Company,
who reported record profits from all
that fancy travel going on. But Daisy,
she went sterling, unadulterated, her son
holding her hand and singing her out.
The song, from America's old songbook,
for the oldest love story in the world.
Mother and child. Daisy and son.
Never mind his sixty years and her ninety-four.
Never mind the platitudes about a long life
well lived. It was mother and son
all over again. Michelangelo's *Pietà*
repeated, and if he could, gray hair, PhD
and all, he'd have crawled into the cold marble
of her lap if only to be close to the womb
he'd come from, that day sixty years ago
when the two of them, laboring all night,
rode the high hills of pain, she behind,
he in front, head down and coming,
the way he is now—pedaling hard
into that first cold slap of mourning.

Inseparable

That's how we girls were back then—
goofy and inseparable, jacked up
on ID bracelets and our own sugar,
gushing hormones like an open hydrant.

Flat-bellied and slender as saplings
joined at the root, we dared
past the timberline, high as heroic
and holding on stubborn. After that
nothing was as good, nothing
as teetering or alive. We were
caffeine without the coffee, juice
without the squeeze, unadulterated
and sure on our little French heels,
until everyone grew up and out of it

but me. Now I'm reduced to talking
to ghosts: Mother, ten years gone
but still in the big green chair tut-
tutting through the pages of her magazine.
Tell me, Frown Face, Breaker of My Heart,
what's for dinner? The stewpot's empty
and all that's left in the cupboard
is your old wet blanket. Sorry to drag
you back, Old Girl, but I'm still so hungry,
and according to your will and the power
of this state I'm in, your wet blanket
and my heart are all I get to chew.

Case #87 on the Calendar

Today Judge Judy is sad.
Not angry, satiric, outraged,
or beside herself. But sad.
The case before her: a couple
married nine years, followed
by an eleven-year separation.
No divorce. Too busy
spying, vandalizing, dragging
each other to court to sue
or countersue. The law's
delight: they cannot stay away
from each other.
               Judge Judy
totals the years. *Twenty, half*
of your adulthood. Live to be
a hundred, and this bitterness
will poison a fifth of your entire
life. Judge Judy is teaching
addition. The Mister coughs.
The wife presses her mouth
into an iron line.
               Judge Judy
fingers her gavel. She wants
this case over. These two can
add as well as she, and logic
is a flimsy rope to burden
the drowned. She persists.
She needs this couple to know
she understands. She needs *us*
to know she understands, for
by virtue of her little lace collar,
she is still a woman and privy

to the pickle flesh is heir to.
She taps into a well of patience
she has little of, planes the edge
of her voice to a kind of kindness:
Cut the knot, get on with your lives,
as if to say, pick up the thread
of who you were prior to this
Gordian snarl, for surely, before
the gavel bangs and the hammering
commercials start, she could cast
on the screen of their imagination
the emerald city of marital order
and good sense. But how much
can one do?

                Judge Judy, don't
be sad. No one could slip a piece
of paper between these two.
They will leave your courtroom
and go on with their lives, just as
you advised, for bitterness *is*
their life—the meat they chew,
the bone they gnaw. It is the pit
of the apricot worked in the mouth
after the sweetness goes. Suck
on *that* long enough and the stone
cracks open to its seed: prussic acid:
amygdalin, otherwise known
as cyanide.

                Arithmetic lesson #2.
If ten apricot seeds can kill a child,
how many will it take to kill love?

Too many to count. I learned that
at my mother's knee—she
who dished it out as well as took it.
*How do you know that's not how
your father and I made love?* So much
for my limp logic. At her knee
I learned it, Judge Judy, her arthritic
knee, trembling to manipulate the
walker. Her ninety-five-year-old knee.

II

Witness

I'm trying to figure out
what the name of that flower
must be. The one leaning toward me,
washed by a thin pencil of falling water
and trembling like a first corsage
on a young wrist bone.

The business of this hour is
remembering what I never knew:
a puzzle that seizes the mind on this mild
spring day, shoving all else aside.

The flower itself—worthy
of a painter's study—shivering
like the last witness in Eden
when Eve gathered the rest in her arms
and escaped through the terrible gates.

First Blood

It was a low stagger to his knees—
the blow no linen could bind,
no scab heal. Rolled up
in the scroll of first narratives,
that story was ours, our script,
our blueprint for tragedy. But
what was the cause, the reason
for the hissy fit that initially
lifted high the club: the straw
that broke a brother's back?

The vagaries of a mother's kiss
or the slap of a crazed father
doomed to live in the loss
of high clover and an apple
on every tree? Or both.
Oh Wanderer—ancestor
of us all who can't go home again—
since you walked this earth, one child
has *always* carried the pain, chewing
on the inside of his cheek, biding his time.

2. ABEL

He was his mother's favorite,
his father's despair and shame. Artless
and simple, content to sleep outside
with the sheep, curled nostril to nostril
breathing in their oblivion.

Unlike his brother, he never learned
to toughen up. His only defense—
the indestructible shield
of his mother's morning kiss
tasting of Eden. *Sweetface,*
she'd call him, running her thumb
down his cheek. *My apple dipped in honey.*

Sometimes while milking or plucking
burrs out of wool, he'd raise his head,
sure he heard the rush of angel wings.
But Cain who knew better, being older,
frowned, saying it was only sparrows
in the hayloft, flitting in and out,
there where the sun gathers its light,
shafting down like an accusing finger.

He did not see the blow coming,
the looming shadow raised above him.

But Christ—who wasn't born yet—watched
from the back of God's eye where he lived,
and saw through the little black hole
this wide-eyed dumbling, a rosy boy

dearer than the lamb he cradled to his chest.
A lamb himself, a mother's darling. The pulse
beating in his neck, throbbing for the sacrifice.

3. SETH

She buried her love for Abel
in the recesses of her heart, then
closed the door. Of the other
she never spoke. When it was time
to begin the begetting, she was given
a replacement. Had she a choice,
she'd have fancied a girl, someone
to talk to. But when had she *ever*
been given a choice? Except—
as Adam kept reminding her—
when that talky fellow, that glittery
creature sidled up to her and . . .

but then the vision fades, shreds
like the tail end of a dream. Besides,
there's dishes to be done and a baby
to be rocked. And if she rocked him
haphazardly—he being a substitute,
a compensation—he didn't seem
to mind. He grew up wiry, healthy.
Kept his room clean, milked the goat,
mucked out the barn. His father
tolerated him. His mother checked
his fingernails before he left for school,
patted his head. Signed his report cards.

What warmth he needed he found
in paper, pencil, and adding things up.
A natural in mathematics and geometric
progressions, reciting to the birds

his beloved multiplication tables
while weeding the garden, hoeing the peas.

But one evening in his fifteenth year
he came home troubled, having watched
the ram ramming against the side slats
of his pen, snorting and sniffing the air.
The ewes restless in the field and itchy.
And he, not able to look away.

He told his story at dinner. His mother
and father looked at each other
then put down their forks.
Somewhere a clock started ticking.
Somewhere a calendar turned a page.
So it was written.
Eve reached to the fruit bowl
in the middle of the table, selected an apple—
Empire red as the inside of God's mouth
and rolled it across to her son.

Dumped at Heaven's Gate

When a hurricane spirals
down, spinning like an unhooked
tongue shrieking in the wind's
wet mouth, beheading trees
and cracking open the sky,

pregnant cows in the fields
let down their calves. Whether
the cause is barometric pressure
or the trauma of a bovine nightmare,
the legs buckle and the great spasms
of the uterine walls begin. All day
and into the night, hit by a fury
of flying leaves and limbs
she labors: a fifteen-hundred-
pound bellow nailed to the spot.
All the world's misery concentrated
in that heaving flesh, that drenched
monolith of quiver and rolling eyes.

And if in the wind's howl and rain,
her warm, slick package manages
to slip out and live, and she—
remembering to turn her head and
lick it clean—blinks to find it next morning
wobbling on first legs, that too is Easter.

Looking Through the Album

Seville's geraniums shouting
from window boxes, flamenco
danced in the streets. Squadrons
of swallows flying over El Greco's
red-tile roof, dipping a salute and blessing.
A scuff of hoof. The medieval fortress
that is Toledo. Córdoba's Great Mosque.
The gypsy caves. *A snort, a scuff of hoof*
pawing in a locked stall. How Spain
never seemed to darken before midnight,
the stars since, never so bright.

See how the brain is driven to paste in
the pictures no camera ever took.

A bullring in Madrid. The sun,
a spotlight. The sky, a pitiless blue.

Even before the matador
spun in his suit of lights, waving
the bloody ear, and the Americans
gathered up their souvenirs in disgust
and left. Yes, even before that business
of beauty and ritual, always the preliminaries—
the gold-coach gawk before a royal wedding,
the frenzy before the sacrifice.

Deafened by banging pots
and trumpets, prodded and stabbed
by a surround of dazzle into a sand-
cloud rage of confusion, the bull
is primed for the cape. But this time—
having had enough—he bellowed out

the betrayal he was bred for,
swayed from right to left, then
lowering his head as if to smell
the bloody next of what was coming,
picked up the picador and his horse—
the whole package—lifted them on his horns
and heaved them over.

Centaur of jab and iron spike,
whose paid job is torment, whose glory
is to drive mad, done for in a tangle
of screams and kicking legs.

No cause/effect. What happens
to the bull is written in the beginning
from the moment he appears—blinded
by light and bedecked in ribbons—
no matter what he does. But that scene
paces in my memory like a caged misery
with nowhere to go or passageway—poetic
or otherwise—to lead it, gently, out.

When did we first

entertain the notion
all this was made for us?
In what B.C. was that?
And who was the thinker
who chewed his nails
down to the bloody quick,
shunning his fields
and his best brown goat
to come up with what
every four-foot, crawly,
leafy thing knows better?

What teeth-shattering
cold coerced him—
rolled up in his nightly rag—
to seek such consolation?

Surely he knew nothing
of us, our smattering
of smarts: smart phones,
smart alecks, smart asses,
smart bombs, and how—
thanks to mischief, may-
hem, and Michelangelo—
we swallowed his line,
happy to agree with him.
Even the skinny kid,
his arm around his girl,
walking the back lane
in this forsaken town,
thinks his pounding heart
the drumbeat of this world.
Never mind the daisies'

argument with Coke cans
and orange peels raging
in the ditch, and overhead
the crows who recognize
human faces—so they say—
and remember.

Judith

The Book would have you believe
she too was touched by God's finger,
virtue stiffening her spine from crown
to heel. Israel's best daughter—paragon
of widowhood—confining herself
for three years and four months
to a back room, praying and fasting,
married now to the needle and the loom.

But when the opportunity came
to get out, she took it. If that meant
butchery on her part, fine. A heartfelt
prayer before and after should take
care of it. Prayer and a little rouge.

When the plan came to her, whole,
as if in a dream, she threw off
her sackcloth, her widow's weeds,
and unlocked the trunks of silks and jewels
stashed in the attic. Silver chains, ankle bells,
and gold, beaten gold to pull in the light
and hold its spotlight to her face—
the face God had given her just for this.

The elders gnawed their knuckles,
twiddled their beards. Holofernes's army
roaring at the gates and not one idea
among them. *A woman, a woman.*
What have we come to? Her eyes,
slit-steel. She clenched her jaw.
They did as she demanded.

How can we say she didn't enjoy it,
knowing she and she alone chose to take
the hilt of history in her own two hands?
Sawing away at the big man's greasy neck,
gambling with her dimpled cleverness
to haul the bloody head home
through enemy lines. To lug it, banging
in its tote against her thigh, oozing
with the sticky evidence of her triumph.

What does a woman feel who gives
herself permission to test the dark depths
of what she is? I see her years later
sitting at her loom, the shuttle
dropped from her hands in an ecstasy
of thought, smirking to remember
how when she returned, covered with
the red juice of slaughter, the elders—
kissing her fingers in all their obsequious
gratitude—couldn't look at her straight
or hide the bloodshot terror in their eyes.

In an August Mirror

Now is the time of ironweed, knotweed,
thistle and heavy heat—simmering and brutal.

Now is the time of no time when all days
rise in the oven the same and go forth in single file.

Ninety-six degrees, a sea of grasses too heat-
stunned to move, and I, standing in their midst—

a foolish woman straining like Odysseus
to hear the sirens sing. When suddenly, there,

from the field's buggy depths of buzz, rustle,
and drone—rubbing legs and scraping wing—

the incessant cry of insatiability, the jittery song
of last chance, last chance. Each note, a letter

of the earth's alphabet. Each note, another stitch
knit into the scarf. Never mind decorations

of goldenrod and doilies of Queen Anne's lace
or the interminable grasses standing upright

and righteous as a society of burning saints.
I know who I am. I know with whom I belong.

Wasps

Last spring, wasps took over
the bluebird house. Squatters
gnawing out the entryway
for the wood and saliva soup
needed for nests. Good
tenants they were too—
clean, quiet, busy: each egg
nestled in its hexagonal crib,
coverlets tucked and tended to.

When the birds arrived, flashing
their blue entitlement, they took
one look and left. We too stayed clear.
Some goings-on one shouldn't
mess with. Motherhood for instance.

Trouble is, that holy state doesn't
last. Lately my son has fallen
for a 1990 BMW, revving her up
to race her. He's installed a roll
cage, head and neck restraints,
wears flame-retardant gloves
and a Nomex bodysuit lest she
combust and finish him off good.

This is the child whose pajamas
caught fire when he was seven,
the child whose layers of skin
I watched curl back black
from the galloping edge of burning,
the gleaming front line of terror.
And now, just when I need it, my old
mother-song of *Like hell you will*

doesn't work anymore. What pedestal
is left for me to stand on? What
good are eyes in back of the head
without the advantage of clout?

He agrees, his laugh ringing me round
the way it always did: seed of my
November, brown-eyed dearest of boys.

I think I need lessons from the wasps,
for am I not also maker of paper nests,
wrought and tended to? And do I not
also feed on nectar and fallen fruit?
O Queen of buzz and sovereign care,
when does one stop gnawing at the heart's hole—
that entryway, that mother price? That sting.

At the Gates

Paris in June and we are in love.
Delacroix, wine, late nights
at the Louvre. *Liberté,
Égalité, Fraternité.* And each
and every morning Camembert
and apricot *confiture* on a hunk
of good French bread—breakfast
in the park. A bench by the lilacs.

The park, *Pour les Enfants*—
a gated, safe place for little ones,
toddlers, chubby-legged preschoolers.
The sign said so.

Vive la France, we thought.

Funny how we never grew tired
watching them—digging in dirt,
spinning in place, or herding ants
with a leaf. The pure concentration
it takes to be two years old: the gravity
of buttonholes, the trembling lip
and pride of holding fast
to one's own red pail and scoop.

On our last morning we saw
another sign, erected in 1945.

1945. The war over. The park
rededicated to *les enfants*
not permitted to enter these gates—
the yellow-starred ones who would
never come back. I see them

clinging to their mothers' skirts,
coveting the swings beyond the iron bars,
the just-their-size merry-go-round,
before *le gendarme* with the frown
and big stick threatens them away.

Add them up. The same ones,
six thousand of them. Babies
ripped from their mothers, howling
in the brutal crush and bedlam
of Drancy—the internment camp
outside Paris, set up and organized
not by Germans but by the French.

Oh, that the tongues of lilac—
those silent witnesses—could speak
a different end to this story.

You, combing hair in the mirror
or engrossed in the evening news.
You, spearing asparagus, anticipating
the meat loaf, the fork shining
like your life, eager and balanced
in your hand. Can you not hear them,
frantic against the gates, whimpering
for their mothers? The big trains
warming on the tracks. What would
you give for your ongoing comfort
to not know what must have been said:

Shh, no crying. Mama's waiting
at the end of this nice train ride.
She'll be standing in front of another
set of gates, oiled to swing wide
and welcome you in. Up you go.

III

Baring the Inevitable

Empty nests rock in the high trees—
blotches against the sky
while the forest pantomimes
in the morning sun a merry dying.

Fall comes to Georgia the way
all seasons come to Georgia.
In a rush. No question as to what's
going on. The spider, the scummy
pond, the blood-red oak. They know.
Owls hoot the news to each other
in the half-light of dusk while mice
shiver in their grasses and holes.

Do not let beauty fool you.
Behind the palette of iridescence,
it's murder that marks these days.
Maybe what the forest is rustling
is *Help*, watching the sky flood down
relentless, filling up its vacancies.
I tell you, we are witnessing a battle
for nakedness, a struggle the leaves
already know has been lost. See how
they tear themselves apart, flashing
their wounds as they fall, whispering
remember me, remember me.

Deep Purple

Monday, and today's job is cleanup.
I'm humming an old song to keep
me company, something about purple
and a garden wall. The children
are concerned, for it was only yesterday
I measured out my future, stretching
greedy-big as open arms could reach.
Now here I am, backsliding into old lyrics.

I'm reminded of a woman I once knew
who loved purple—not lavender, that sickly
excuse—but deep purple. She wore it,
painted the inside of her house with it,
her lips, her nails, the bottom of her pool
where she'd spend long afternoons floating
in tinted water. She claimed she didn't
know the song, neither words nor tune,
written before her time, but there, behind
her eyes, behind her studied cheerfulness,
it must have existed. Not the doo-wop version
that ruined it, but the old one that a patched-up
woman might have a need for.

I know, this has little to do with cleaning,
except to say her house was spotless,
not a thing out of place, as if she spent
each morning shoving back in a back closet
too deep for any rag to reach, a memory.
I want to think it was about love. About
a cherished someone sucked prematurely

out of this world, draining away like
a slow twilight into the ground. A lingering
subtraction that left her lost, wandering
in deep purple, nightshade, and sorrow.

ℒ Is for Leaves

Not to worry. Each morning
after you kiss my cheek
and lock the door behind you,
leaving me alone with my body
and this house to walk it around in,
I've plenty to do. Monitoring
the meat defrosting on the counter,
checking the refrigerator light's
on and off, and periodically
resuming my post by the window
to count the leaves, it being August
and there are so many.
                                    I imagine
you've not noticed, rattling
your car keys, eager to get going,
but there they are in their summer
uniforms—cheek to cheek like well-
behaved children at choir camp
and all looking in at me looking out
at them.
              Often I think they look
to spirit me away, chattering
among themselves the way they do,
at times getting quite agitated
as if they have something of import
to tell. Of course you'd say it's only
the breeze, and you're probably right—
you always are—so it's better I not
admit how I drop whatever I'm doing
to position myself by the window
and tap on the glass, signaling back

to show I'm paying attention.

                                    Usually
it's sunny and they're only swinging
in blue air, yet they do want me to watch
the way the children did when we'd
take them to the park in the old days.
But when the clouds unlock, roaring in
dark and furious, and the tossing
gets vindictive—the hail needling down
cold as ridicule, their little faces slapped
into a panic, twisted on their necks,
and the battering starts—I'm nose pressed,
hands splayed against the glass, not knowing
which of us is screaming, *Hold on, hold on.*

Putting Two and Two Together

First they dragged the night table
out from between the twin beds and
quietly quietly pushed them together,
then, careful to avoid a noise, lay down
under the ceiling fan, giving in
to the sweet flooding of the flesh.
After, they joked about the plastic tree
in the corner, how, playing Adam and Eve,
that dusty relic must be a stand-in, not for
the wisdom tree but for the other: God's tree,
lest they eat and live happy forever.

This, the opening page of a longer story
begun in a rented room of love talk
and muffled cry. A far cry (or was it?)
from the original story: that sixth-day,
once-upon-a-time story when the earth
cracked, spewing forth all manner of beast
and crawly, creeping thing. Imagine
the noise, the bellows and bleats, the thunder,
the hammering rain to make the mud to make
the man, slashed by a burning fork of lightning
in his side, the woman screaming to get out.

Anniversary

It was a slow dying: a knife
not plunged in but meandering
toward its mark as if it could not
figure out death's entrance. A straying
of the will we left behind in the room
we had abandoned, masquerading as
a photograph or an old brass lamp
to rub that might have saved us.

But how could anything have saved us?

Not in a sailor suit like any other boy
when you were six, but decked out
in the stiff white uniform of an admiral—
your mama's little man. How could I
compete with that? Even when I met you,
twenty-five and old before your time.
Not enough galoshes and mufflers
in the world to hold you in it.

(I don't want to write this)

Today—fifty years to the day—we would
have been one of those photographs
in the style section of the newspaper.
Me, stiff-lipped. You, as yet unscathed
in a la-dee-da future of perfectly starched shirts
and the twenty years of handkerchiefs I pressed,
just so, for your breast pocket.

Now you wear a dirt shirt. In spring
a boutonniere of dandelions. Always the dresser!

Taking a Turn with Sappho

Peitho of the white doves, child of Aphrodite, was the goddess
of persuasion sung to at bridal feasts by the maidens

and mother-in-law as they pushed the bride into the chamber
where he waited. And maybe there were cushions and a couch

and a little weeping to be done before he lifted her veil
and eased her down onto the sheets perfumed with flowers.

All night her companions sang outside the locked door
while *his* entourage shouted encouragement. I imagine

it was early February, the wedding time in Greece when
trees were fit to bursting—groaning with sap—while leaves

and blossoms, still dormant, lay rigid in their overcoat of bark.

The Descent

Like a valentine, they stood
silhouetted against the sunset
then made jokes about the sun
looking like a runaway cheese
which made them laugh
and freed them from the love talk
the moment seemed to require.

At first, the fall was merry,
delicious in a way—that shuffle and trip,
riding the slick of language down
from boredom by way of disparagement
to distance. To disaster.

What they'd remember later was dusk
and the two of them standing at the railing
in the growing darkness
which shocked them at first—
the light had been so beautiful—and then
the silence and the sudden reaching out
to hold hands, like victims of the Triangle Fire
holding hands as they jumped.

Metamorphosis

Before she died, my mother
practiced turning herself into stone.
Now she sits—a rock on my father's grave,
six feet above his reach. Each spring
he punches a hole in his roof,
sending up a riot of yellow flowers
to tempt her into softening. The tendrils
of his need claw the air, grope to touch her,
but she will have none of it.

The sun goes up, comes down.
Nothing changes. I've walked this
manicured lawn, its straight and narrow
in a wrap-around of grief long enough.
I've tried to lift her, move her
to where he's not, but she's become
too heavy for my scraped arms to hold.

Maybe after walking this earth for
ninety-five years, she should be allowed
to turn into whatever she wants.
Not just a stone but a boulder
flaunting bulk and weight. A sumo
wrestler of a boulder, bristling
and unyielding. The Rock of Gibraltar—
that frowning monolith born to guard
the Mediterranean's western gate
and blot out the sun. That mother rock,
beyond which—those ancient Greeks said—
you fall off the earth.

Clytemnestra, Unleashed

Lovingly, she poured the scented
water into his bath, helped him off
with his robe, planting little kisses
across his back, then shot the bolt home
and went at him with an axe. His left foot
she grabbed first, then sloshing forward
on her knees, crawled over the fallen
mountain of his body, hacking away.
When the job was done, she stood before
the palace doors, dripping righteous
in the red evidence of her vengeance.

Always the simmering question—
what to do with her life, the endless
waiting for what the oracle promised,
what the stars writ large. One thing
she knew: the jailhouse pacing
on the parapets would stop, the dry
winds from the east that brought no news
would stop. For now at last, the giddy
joy of action: breathing hard, the sticky
handle of the chopper she'll not put down.

Curse by curse, rattle by rattle,
the press of bones piled up behind her,
scraping and jostling for attention.
Time to clean out this house.
Sacrifice for sacrifice, murder for murder.

Her lover hid in the closet. The deed,
he said, being *woman's work*.

Who could blame her?
Even the Grand Coulee Dam—
holding back and filled to choking—
would crack, groan, and yawn open.
It's anger that leaps and rages, foaming
through the rift, churning the carcass
of a life into a high red boil of blood.
Woman's blood. Unclenched, unyielding,
and unbuttoned. You better believe it.

On This May Morning

for Lillian

Clear-eyed daughter of winter, born
on the coldest night of the year,

now is the time to walk this earth
lightly, for now is the season of catkin

and fluff, flute song and chirp—
the yearly reenactment of beginnings

when earth deploys in her new green
uniform to reclaim her old address.

Walking by the river, past squirrel
scurry and chat and a box turtle stuck,

stymied in traffic, I stop at a smear—
a trace of some unfortunate

dried out and graying on the path.
Above it, a spray of honeysuckle

bends heavy to see, weeping perfume
from its profusions. Nature's joke.

Nothing means what we want it to mean.
Yet child, dearest child, named for the lily

burgeoning hope in the quickening ground
and for a grandmother whose Yiddish name,

your name, translates as *love*, I tell you,
the lies we embrace to endure this world

are delicate. Be careful where you walk.

The Hike

Using roots as steps to steady me,
I climbed the steep trail. Early June.
Already the forest bristling with brush,
and from some leafy nook, a thrush
to *rinse and wring* as Hopkins said.
Okay, maybe not a thrush. I don't know
my birds, but I know an empty mailbox
pleading for a note when I hear it. Then,
like flutes in competition for first chair
or, better, a duet of star-crossed lovers,
two birds sang their love song, cycling
through the trees enough *rinse and wring*
to open a laundromat. So I drove home
blissful in my blue car with a stick shift,
a stick because I like to feel I'm really
driving the thing, ate a cheese sandwich
on gluten-free and pondered how to work
that bird song into a poem called "Spring"
the way Hopkins did because it made him
so happy, so happy he said before he died.
I bet he was thinking of the thrush. I know
I was. I tell you, I mulled a long time
about the best way, the most honest way,
to compose my poem. The challenge
to put everything in, no cheating allowed.
Thrush, car, the Swiss cheese sandwich.
Instead, I diddled around and watched
a show on cable about birds, featuring
David Attenborough who always seems
so happy, hiking the jungles of Paraguay
to find the only three-feathered bird
in existence. Not like me, plodding the
streets of Dublin looking for Glasnevin

where Hopkins is buried only to find
it closed. So I conjured up my thrush
who lives in the fourth line of this poem,
and pressing my head to the locked gates,
squeezed out a thought: maybe Hopkins'
thrush was really Whitman's lilac bird
and Hardy's darkling rolled into one,
born to sing, luminous and indelible, for all
the world's troubled poets. Even for me.

IV

November Trees

The forest doesn't bury its dead
but stands among them—
last year's leaves curled at its feet,
the fallen logs of its kind.

If the trees murmur or sigh,
crack or groan,
it is only the wind.
The trees themselves are silent.

In all their grace
and terrible nakedness they symbolize
nothing. They are beyond us.
How can we bear it?

Dark Sky

Storming.
Three weeks straight now.
Our surrounding forest—
the wrap-around rock
and refuge we live in—
thrashes in desperation,
struggling in the running mud
to maintain a foothold.

When the winds whip up
we flee to the basement
armed with flashlight and radio,
hold our breath at each slow
rip giving up at the root.
We do not look at each other
straight, imagining every tilt
and crash, earth groaning open,
leaving behind a gaping O,
raw as any mother's mouth,
having lost her child.

Who says
earth doesn't weep—
its canopy of cardinal heaven
shaken by the throat into patches?

What Pollyanna business is this
about respite: hint of stray starlight
and the heroic song of one wet bird?
The damage is done. Between storms
the only sound is the leaves' *drip drip:*
Morse code for sorrow, for incomprehensible,
for one more blow coming through.

High Country, First Night

The smell of all-night rain
    drunk on the breath of mountain laurel
        oozes through the screens.

And I, stuck in a dream I can't get out of,
    struggle to fill a bottomless suitcase,
        intent on going somewhere.

Breakfast at this cabin's hand-me-down table,
    the knife suddenly frozen in my hand,
        for I can't get over the fact

that where I was going was here, and how
    in sleep the mind's job is traveling
        to get you where you already are.

Morning sun spears the forest canopy,
    but last night hangs on, dripping
        from the eaves. A ticking clock.

Not the new kind of clock where one number
    swallows down the last in silence:
        blink, and one more second of your life

is gone without even an accompanying
    tick of elegy. Nature keeps time
        the old-fashioned way—slow,

lugging its luggage of leaves through seasons
    the way the mind drags its baggage
        through nights' endless terminals,

struggling to catch up while preserving
  what it has. The way oak keeps its leaves
    through winter. The way here, in this

drenched green privacy, blossoms
  of mountain laurel—cluster-heavy and
    drowning in rain—begin their surrender,

giving in to the soft, brown inevitable
  eating away at their edges.
    Each cup trembling to hold on to its drop.

Speaking of Belief

Somehow the mimosa,
chopped down in all her grace,
has produced an heir. The stump
has delivered a twig: a wee surrogate
big in bravery, tribute to no one
but a dead mother who believed.

This faith business, a mama's job.
Each berry quickening on a stem—
testament. Past the crabbing, every
teenage tantrum, new clothes
balled up littering the floor, still
the mother forges on. Even
after her death, rattling in the brain
for good or ill, witness or cop,
sympathizer or the never-to-heal
cut of *I told you so*. But always
the voice. Blood is blood.

What other offer is there?

The Toad

Yesterday I found a desiccated toad,
sucked out and weightless.

Each toe—long, curved,
delicate as eyelash. The twin
eye sockets, the slit of the mouth,
the froggy bend of the back knees
flexed to jump. Only the insides
were missing. The wet batteries
of the body's workings. The juice.
The amazing tongue.

Like the princess in a tale,
I carried it upstairs.

In what hour of the night
and by whom
was the deed done? the slurp
of flesh drained out as if drawn
by a straw, leaving a carapace
for the sun to mummify
on my doorstep.

I am waiting for the toad
to answer. Shell of a stolen life,
empty as a dinner plate, empty
as the sky that looked down
on the making of this knick-knack,
this siphoned-out perfection.

Gently I placed the toad
on my pillow. Do not laugh.
I expect much from the dead.

Unlike the princess who never
sat waiting in a hospice room,
I've had practice, kissing the silent,
vacant clay—warts and all.

Late Night Conversation

from Levertov's "The Opportunity"

My father, after his death,
appeared to me in a dream. Not
as a rose or young boy as you say
yours did, but wearing his own face.
He came only once, the night after
I buried Mother. He came to take her,
to lead her to the bed next to him,
to lay her down and pretend—
as she had always done—that she
liked it that way.
                   What stop sign
could I have raised against him?
What magic flower, what words?
He always knew she'd come, the way
she always did when he did a naughty
and needed scolding—her bad, bad boy.

In your poem, your father
returns as a child of six, allows
a kiss and brief embrace. The dream
emerges from the sea. The child's body
part of it—alive in the vast, plumed endlessness.

I envy your poem and your father.
I envy your dream where the towering
walls of water that come and come
deliver no old wounds soaked in salt
to fester again
                but deliver instead
an invitation to wade in, arms open

to greet the watery ghost. A ghost come
simply because your name was daughter,
and all traces of a dingy underlayer
washed clean and white as bone.

The Engagement Ring

The woman sitting in front of me
has auburn hair whirling in a cowlick—

helicopter hair that wears the mark
of the pillow all day—the hair that will

not lie down. Her roots, asphalt gray,
as if at the bottom of that spiral,

she's already been anointed by dust.
Yet here she sits, listening to poetry

and the expert's lecture, taking notes
as if life went on forever, as if that

swirl at the back of her head were not
the promise of the patient one who keeps

her company all night, fiddling with her hair.
How quiet he must be, knees tucked,

his soft breath blowing open the space
to place his lipless kiss. Look how

she periodically raises her hand
to pat the back of her head the way

a woman does, checking the state
of her hair. Or perhaps she's uneasy,

feeling my eyes riveted to the spot.
Or like the newly betrothed, she can't

help herself, drawn to the unfamiliar
gravity of it, twisting it around her finger—

the ring that is, and what it means: the pull
of the vortex, the signature of forever.

White Blood

Roses climb[ed] his life as if he were their trellis.
—WILLIAM H. GASS

Of his diagnosis, Rilke writes only
of the cause: *the prick of a rose,*
recalling that cut on his left hand
while gathering roses for Nimet,
the Egyptian beauty. The initial
infection spreading from one arm
to the other. But who knows
how many years prior to that
stab and subsequent agony,
white cells began multiplying
in the corridors of his veins?

Imagine, Narcissus in spats
clutching the pain gnawing
under his waistcoat, running
a tongue over his mouth's
ulcerous sores. See how he
bends to the haze of his breath
lingering on the pool's mirror
as if like a rose or poem, breath too
demands to be committed to memory
before it lifts and melts away.

Roses in a silver bowl. Red rags
rioting the June fences, or upright
in a crystal vase. Roses delivered
in florist paper or stolen from
a neighbor's garden, but always
the glistening contradiction:
death alive in the bud, alive

in the terrible beauty
of the rose's bite. Could he
have come any closer to you, *Angel,*
than to this deepest self, pressed
in a book or left behind like a limp
reminder on a window sill?

When he said, *all soarings*
of my mind begin in my blood,
how could he not have known?
Twenty-five years before his death,
almost to the day, he paced the cliffs
at Duino—waves crashing the rocks,
bleeding out their white blood,
row after row pricked from within
by the white goad that rises in the body—
the thorn in the flesh wanting out.

Oh, what difference now.

To a dying poet, secrets matter little.
The high hour belongs to death:
the body's auger, the egg tooth
carried with us from the day we're born.
The white bit drilling its inexorable
way through the shell to the gift
we in our solitude always wanted to be:
the everlasting rose that mattered.

Reading Boccaccio

A kissed mouth doesn't lose its freshness:
like the moon it turns up new again.

So says *The Decameron,* still teaching
after six hundred years. How many
mouths can one book inspire in six
centuries? A hundred a day if lips
are eager and the moon is shining.
Do the math. That's over twenty-two
million—Ohio and Illinois combined.
I say *Read.* With practice, you could
be the Johnny Appleseed of Kisses,
meandering the Midwest, knee-
deep in corn, perpetually puckered.
Who wouldn't greet you at the gate?
Clear a path through the fields
to reach one whose mouth turned up
fresh and new all the time?

When I was still fresh and new,
rising slender as a sliver each dawn
from my innocent bed, what did I know
of kisses before there was Kenny—
Picklehead my sister called him—
boy of loose limbs and red hair
who sang when we danced.
But the night he finally bent to me
and trotted out his kiss, what I got
was a rake of teeth, a hit-and-run
collision of the mouth. What I wanted

was to be ruined, to fling back my head
in an unbearable sweetness, what Boccaccio
must have known with his Fiammetta in the garden
at the end of the seventh story, second day.

Donatello's Prophet

Museo dell'Opera del Duomo, Firenze

Here stands Habakkuk, plain as a post.
No adornment, no iconography—
book or scroll—to explain himself.
The marble drapery—from a sculptor
who could fold and pleat stone
with the best of them—economical.
The body, ascetic—stringy neck,
sparse of hair. The feet, veiny, size
twelve, not an ounce of fat between them.

But in the bare bulbs of the eyes,
the sculptor has struck a madhouse look,
born from an urgency that leans
the statue forward, burning with
something to say. So realistic that
when finished, Donatello, with one
whack of the chisel, opened the prophet's
mouth, and stepping back and away,
shouted, *Speak, damn you, speak.*

Whether the statue delivered or not
I don't know. Donatello never said.
But I say, *this* Habakkuk's speech
would have spewed out rigid as his
stone dress, chilling as his own
chapter and verse. The marble
tongue, locked in the dark recesses
of his mouth for so long, with nothing
to suck on but censure and woe:

Woe unto him that saith to the wood 'Awake,'
To the dumb stone, 'Arise!'

Ah Donatello—genius of hammer,
chisel, polish and gleam—were not
those words the flung gauntlet?
The slap in the face? Freshly anointed
in marble dust, birthing tools still hot
in your hands, you'd have stared him down—
triumphant. Was not that frenzy of flying
chips your answer? your vindication?
Your ten paces, turn, and shoot?

Ammunition

for D.H.

My childhood home didn't have
guns from three wars mounted
on the walls as yours did. We had

other weapons. We learned early
how to hone in on the soft parts
without all that metal. We had eye-

darts and below-the-belt ridicule.
We had a stick-it-to-you-you'll-
never-get-rid-of-it shiv in the ribs.

So I'm not impressed by your
Antiques Roadshow collection
of flintlocks and Smith & Wessons,

Great-Grandpa's blunderbuss. Nor
do I envy your born-into-it flags,
rebel yells, and "honorable causes."

My ammo's smeared with older blood,
rue blood, Jew blood, so much blood
the world's sick of hearing about it.

One look at that lady in the harbor
raising a torch to her own platitudes
and we thought we could forget

the malice we'd been taught. Why not?
A new leaf in the book, a new page,
a new start in this America, this

streets-paved-with-gold America
of pushcarts and factory piecework.
Tell me, Friend, you with the guns,

what other true-blue Americana
decked your walls? We had Roosevelt.
Franklin Delano. A grinning photo

of the man who was going to save us.
Trouble was, he couldn't save us. Nothing
could save us. Not even the six million

he let slip through his fingers. Six million,
shot, starved, or up the chimney, to add
to our stockpile for future use. Their DNA

roiling down the gutters of Brooklyn,
up the broad avenues of Manhattan,
and across the Hudson to follow us

wherever we went. No, we never had
stashes of guns. We had violins and books.
And if we had to hide or hightail it and run,

we took what we could with us. Sure,
we gave America corned beef on rye,
lox, bagels, and George Gershwin.

Not to mention the Salk vaccine, cheese
danish and Phil Levine. You can't say
we weren't generous. But don't be fooled.

We had weapons. And we could dish it out with the best of them. Ice-Pick Willie had nothing on us. He used a gun. We used guilt.

V

Of Mischief and the Moon

The door cracks a knife-edge open.
Temptation puckers for a kiss,
and I—on automatic
and sharp as an old appetite—
shove my way through,
slamming the door behind me.
Now here I am on the wrong side,
unable to get back.

Mother shakes a bony finger
from the grave. *Now you've done it!*

Oh, if only I could drain this day out
and pour a fresh one in it, wake
myself up before this morning's sun
and crawl out of a blameless bed.

Don't laugh. There's precedent
for this. Once a month the moon
takes a holiday, vanishes for days,
hides, claims she's resting—
all that heavy-duty wax and shine.
Why can't I do the same? Lie low.
Pretend what happened didn't.
Take a potion, a pill, and come out
new again. A debutante, a mere
sliver of a girl, delicate as an eyelid
winking to my sidekick—my evening
star, my Venus—who always was a liar.
Baby, don't desert me now. Be my acolyte,
my votive candle. Focus your bright light
here where everyone can see me
posing in my little slip of innocence.

Portrait of Poet in Stroller and Awe

Honey-haired and apple-cheeked,
I am four. Bundled up, going store
to store down St. Nicholas. Mother
in her black coat trimmed in fur, hat
cocked over one eye. We are shopping.

Frischling's for farmer cheese and eggs.
The Appetizing Store for sauerkraut
forked up, dripping from the barrel.
Pete's Italian Market where sea bass
and snapper thrash in a too-small vat
before the hit on the head, the icy
bed of one-eye-up laid out like jewels.

But it's the butcher's opening bell
that calls me back. The rack of knives
and polished grinder. Axes and saws.
The shining wand of the sharpener—
its slither sound of steel licking steel.
The ancient writing of the butcher block
streaked with cuts and sacrifice. White apron,
hand-wiped and stiff with a day's red work.
Jelly-globs of liver in a white enameled pan.
Chicken guts pulled out and dumped.
Sawdust on a clean floor and the honest
working hands—blunt-fingered and stained.

No plastic wrap or Styrofoam trays.
Just blood and bone. And Mother—content
only with perfection—flicking a bit of lint
off her sleeve, biting her lip, eyeing the scales.

The Doll

1.

Cloth body. Wooden head
with painted marcelled hair
and painted eyes. Blink
and they were brown.
Like me she was—brown hair
brown eyes—but better. White
dimity frock with pink rosette.
Rosy knees and socks of lace.
Sister named her *Ugly. Her eyes
wider than her mouth. Miss Ugly.*
Her mouth wore dimples. Pursed.
I was five. I knew her worth.

Mama Mama she used to weep
when I'd lay us down to sleep
pray to God my soul to keep
and if I die before I wake
                    and when I woke
and sat her up—brown hair and eyes.
Same body, same white dress
with pink rosette. Same smell.

I'd feed her with a dolly spoon,
touch her lips, count one two three
then eat the food myself.
Sister laughed. Mother hid her face.
What mystery is transubstantiation
when you are five? I knew love.
I understood.
                    Then around her mouth
a hurt, a sore that wouldn't heal.

That is, the paint around her mouth—
an ugly sore that spread. Fixed
was all I wanted. A dab of paint.
How Mother iodined my knee. So what
if she were scarred and wore a mark.
I knew love and understood.

And so I laid me down to sleep,
prayed to God her soul to keep
and should she die before I wake
                        and when I woke—
same body. Same beloved dress.
Same smell. But the head was wrong.
The skin too white.
The hair not brown but black.
And when I sat her up, my baby's eyes
of painted brown flew open—glass
and glittered at me, blue.

2.

The trouble is I never understood.
Shame on you. Look how bad
you made your father feel
who went out of his way
to take a doll to a real hospital
just to make you happy. And look.
She has blue eyes, blue eyes.
Any other little girl in the world
would be thrilled with blue eyes
instead of brown instead of brown
and a new head a new head a new head.

How dare I not be happy
when so much depended on it?

3.

Next scene: flip the pages
of fifty-eight more years.
See my father—Mister Blunder
the mess-up kid—dead
in a hospice room. My father
who used to wash his face
with such a smack and joyful noise
then slick his auburn hair.

Whose head is this—
this bald and toothless wonder?
I examine the neck for transplant,
the line of the old switcheroo.
And I think, maybe if I search
I could find his other head—
his Daddy head—the way years later
I found my doll's in a grocery sack
back of Mother's closet. But then
where to store this one?
In what closet? what paper bag?

Old-man doll on a pillow,
clutching in an icy fist your last
dim handful of heat, your nose
poking up in terror as if you died
smelling your last breath coming, tell me.

Playing Favorites

You ask how I feel about my body,
    my parts. When I was young I loved
        my legs. Ah, the places they carried me—

long legs, lovely legs. How I'd fling them
    about, wrap them around. Don't ask.
        Later, I favored my teeth, especially

after I almost lost them, hitting my face
    on the steering wheel, seeing stars.
        Of course there's the ongoing affair

with hair. Who's not guilty of that?
    But now as I'm getting on in years,
        I admit a certain fondness for my belly.

I call her my cheese. Such a comfort.
    So easy to maintain—no plastic wrap
        or refrigeration necessary. Notice,

I do not speak of insides which tend
    to monitor themselves, only my outer
        delineations which, I'm proud to say,

are immortalized in art. The Louvre,
    the Uffizi, the National Gallery.
        In niches or blazing from the wall—

Venuses, Graces, Muses—boulder girls
    fattened on glory. Wear sunglasses.
        Stand in front of any one of Rubens'

hefty beauties, proud of her dimpled
    cellulose and pudding flesh. And see,
        front and center in all her excess—

my belly. That gurgling pillow, that buttoned
    happiness—creamy soft, homegrown
        and spongy. My big mozzarella.

I tell you, if I could bend myself in half
    I'd eat me for lunch with a slice of tomato
        on a hunk of focaccia or good French bread.

Carried Away

The Rapture must have been cancelled.
The only sudden flight I've seen
belongs to the bird nesting in my begonias
who takes off each time I open the door.
Too bad. I was sure I'd be chosen: popped
out of my comfort zone and sent
spinning like a fluff into space, ejected
from my rocker, ejected from my shoes,
and if you think the Ineffable doesn't have
a sense of humor, my clothes. The crack
of doom and all that. And I'm rising
in a column of fire—all the wane
and wax of my days melting off and away
until like a naked wick vibrating my string
I soar into the arms of Orion. So what
if the pot roast scorches on the stove,
and Grandma, locked frantic in the bathroom,
ends her days jiggling a knob? A favorite
is a favorite. Why shouldn't it be me, picked
for the big prom in the sky, queen of the blue
gymnasium decorated with stars. No dress,
no corsage. The only embellishment, a wee
spark for the bellybutton, enabling me
to fit into the whirling void of the empyrean,
filling gaps in the zodiac so that those left behind
can look up and read the little of what's left
of their fortunes while admiring my beatific shine.

Ars Poetica in a Tilted Chair

Twice a year, Amy the dental hygienist
hovers over me, probing for treasure.
Titanium scraper, hooked mirror, saliva
ejector, water squirter, all vying for space
in the dark recesses of my privacy.
                               She chatters
(this being Georgia) about her chickens,
keeping me up to date. And I, bibbed
and locked in a cranky silence, take refuge
in what the great Flaubert said: *We are all
caged birds . . . eagles or canaries, parrots
or vultures,* which leads me to the conclusion
that, being a poet, I qualify as a chicken:
wing-clipped, cooped up, scratching at dirt.
A silly, flailing about without a head
and hooked on rubbing words together—
my pebbles in a crop. I'm reminded
of Demosthenes, that marbled Greek
who, too, used pebbles, stuffing them
in his mouth to cure a speech impediment
while practicing his oratory, pacing the shoreline,
reciting verses to the sea.
                          Suddenly, the hygienist
interrupts my reverie. She's telling of the day
the last chicken died—mauled by fox or cat,
the splotch of bloody feathers in the yard—
and already I'm writing this poem
while she's pulling the last string of floss
through my teeth, having been given
a new set of pebbles to worry and grind.

Rumba

No one does the rumba the way
those two used to do it—eyes
half closed, the rolling hips speaking
all language necessary, and we
who knew nothing beyond plucking
daisies and pining, stood spellbound,
for there was that dress she wore,
tight with a sheen, plum red, and he,
all slicked-back auburn. Friday night
at the Y with a live band and *It's Romeo*
we'd whisper to each other whenever
he'd walk her onto the floor, making
the gym spark like holy ground
and we, backing up to form a circle
around them respectfully, and why not,
for weren't we true believers, or would be
in a few years, believers not in them
but in the language beneath the music
bodies are born to speak, the language
that hit me like a brick three years later
at my desk where I hid in the back row
of Italian 102 when the professor
leaning over his lectern began reciting
Italian poetry, maybe Cesare Pavese
or Eugenio Montale, who knows,
for I rarely did homework or as little
as possible, and maybe I was supposed
to be translating as he spoke the lines,
but how could I, watching him bend
to the need in us, his eyes half closed—
an invitation not to be refused—and I
who didn't understand a word found
I could suddenly read not the Italian

which was music but underneath it
to where he led with his mellifluous voice
that to me was the silk wrapping
around the *real* words that wound around
the small of my back like an irresistible arm
leading me onto the floor, and I tell you,
I who scrimped on homework and ended up
with a D, learned then how to move
past the ABC of the box step in order
to follow him and those words all my life.

The Poet

He was the right words
in the right order on demand,
the hot blab of the poetry circuit.
So we promised him dinner,
publicity, and a powerful pull
at the punch bowl. We would have
thrown in Italy, rumba lessons, bought
him exclusive, elusive martyr rights
if only he'd come, read his poems
for our little group, disciplined
in nothing but midwest adoration.

He was a Name. What sneer
hadn't he perfected? The arched
eyebrow, the purple scarf, the right
of the rake's progress through
the field of ingenues swaying
before him: children of the corn
facing the blades of the combine.

Over dinner we talked poetry,
influences, whom he read.
His short list of favorites? He
and himself, as if Yeats never
put pen to paper, Shakespeare
wasn't Shakespeare, and poor Keats
never hatched a poorer nightingale.
Frost, Neruda, Rilke—forget it.
"No women?" we said, "Sappho,
Dickinson, Levertov?" He choked
on his fish.
                    Reader, lest I sound
out of joint, I offer up only

what memory shakes out,
and if memory shakes out bitter,
be assured it remains clear-eyed.

He diddled his fork, wiped
his mouth, then, surveying
the table and not finding what
he was looking for, looked down
as if conferring with his plate:
Where's the woman?

No, not a Barrett to banter
with his Browning—alter ego
and companion—but a gate
of female flesh, swung open, wide
and generous. A paltry wage
for genius, yes, but what can be
expected from volunteer work
done flat on the back and provided?

*Sing, O Muse, the cockiness
of the Y chromosome: sole proprietor
of the poetry gene—that itch, that
flea strutting to the podium to be born.*

He read from his "work in progress,"
shuffling, dropping papers, attending
diligently to the fuss of his scarf.
And I wish—for art and the poetry
we kept dangled before us, glittery
as the fruit of Tantalus because
we wanted it so bad—I wish
I could rewrite this story, saying

no one nodded off or walked out,
saying the big man's poems were enough
to fly us beyond judgment's orbit
to where the real stars burn. Their work,
more than bright enough to render the least of them
forgivable. I wish I could tell you that.

S-I-T-Y

That was the word that did me in.
Fourth grade, first one out, red-
faced and back to my seat. Smartest
kid in the class and here comes
that whoops out of my mouth as if
I didn't live on Wadsworth Avenue
and 191st Street in the testosterone
capital of the world and wasn't born
knowing how to spell it.
　　　　　　　　So I grew up,
bought a pair of sneakers, packed
a duffel, and went. And now, from
the high hill of my age, I tell you,
there's concrete to walk, buildings
to gawk, and as many municipalities
to fall in love with as can fill a life.
What else would you want to do
on your last, hard bed but recollect
in tranquility as the Great Daffodil
himself did, even though he never
saw Arequipa of the white stone or
Palermo's trash and blowing papers.
No, he walked the Alps for weeks
on the Stockalper Trail, taking one
extra pair of socks and no change
of underpants, and that's how we
got *The Prelude,* but he never saw
Athens, spread out around a jewel
on a hill. Nairobi, Tangier—see,
I can spell them all. Edinburgh,
Perth—beacon of light—glittering
in the reflection of the Swan River

that wears it for a necklace, like love.
Nor did the old bone ever poke around
cobblestone alleys where desperation
hawks homemade bracelets, and boys
offer a sister for cigarettes or a meal.
Arusha. Santander. Toledo. Open towns,
closed towns with locked gates and walls
twelve feet thick. Bullet-scarred, those too,
and ancient ones like Knossos where
you can run your hand over the fire line,
the fire that destroyed it. Think Delphi
where hunks of broken marble lie about
like *splendor in the grass*. Don't tell me
I don't know my metropolitan areas
and how to spell them. Don't tell me
to sit down again and not get up.

Knee High

Whether squatting,
standing, or stomping
to some mossy memory
on the radio, the knee
takes the brunt. A heart
may pump a million barrels
of blood in a life, enough
to fill three supertankers,
but the knee in its pocket
of synovial fluid proves
the workhorse. It gets us
here to there—Baryshnikov
leap or the bottle-boozy
stagger out of a gutter.
*Fish gotta swim, birds
gotta fly,* as the song goes
and good for them, but I say
the knee is the one joint—
bruised, buckling or bum—
that *scrapes* by. What's
needed? Lyrics about knees,
stable, or teetering and waiting
for the guy wires of muscle
and tendon to steady and lock
making baby good to go.

So sing, O Muse, of the sacred
joint—the meniscus, cartilage,
socket and ball. Nose follower,
bicycle pumper, sally forther,
paired, capped and hinged
to take us the only way
it knows how—straight ahead.

In Praise of Wandering

Iceland

You ask how we do it. Simple.
We travel light. Our stash—peanut butter,
jelly, bread. When we can get it, cake.
We're not fussy. A clean knife
is when I lick it. A *very* clean knife?
We both lick it. Noon, we start
looking for a picnic table or flat rock.
Midges or bad weather, we eat in the car.

This time, the car's name, front and back,
DDX75. A wee car, baby car, raised
on Iceland's clean air, sucking it in
like arctic milk. Our wheels of fortune
bouncing the lupine-lined roads,
riding the gravel ruts of the highlands,
battling the ocean-driven winds. A car,
white as the snowpacks of the interior
and as dear to us as the waterfalls,
the wild swans, and the redshank
with orange legs who chip chip chips
loud enough to drown any murmurs
that might leak out through a keyhole
or under a door.
                    Reader, you may ask,
what door, what murmurs, and where
have these lines taken us, or the car,
parked now on a side street, basking
in Iceland's twenty-four-hour light show
they call a day. If there's a message
to squeeze from this poem of wandering,
it's to be awake to what makes it possible.

And to the sun that makes all things
possible: our beloved battery that spins
in place and never wanders, ever ready
to hold a spotlight steady for us to love in.

ACKNOWLEDGMENTS

I wish to thank the editors of the following journals, in which many of these poems first appeared:

Alaska Quarterly Review: "Dark Sky"

American Journal of Poetry: "Ammunition," "On This May Morning," and "The Descent"

Connotations Press: An Online Artifact: "Case #87 on the Calendar"

Ekphrasis: "Reading Boccaccio" and "Donatello's Prophet"

Georgia Review: "*L* Is for Leaves," "Of Mischief and the Moon," "White Out," "High Country, First Night," "From the Book of Accounts," "Lady Macbeth," and "Portrait of Poet in Stroller and Awe"

Gettysburg Review: "S-I-T-Y," "Once Upon a Time," "Carried Away," "The Engagement Ring," and "Judith"

Grist: "The Poet"

Juxtaprose: "Inseparable"

Lake Effect: "The Hike"

The MacGuffin: "Rumba"

Missouri Review: "Late Night Conversation"

Negative Capability Press: "White Blood"

New Letters: "At the Gates," "Witness," "*Ars Poetica* in a Tilted Chair," "Drawing the Triangle," and "Looking Through the Album"

Ploughshares: "Metamorphosis"

Plume: "In Praise of Wandering" and "Clytemnestra, Unleashed"

Poetry East: "Asking Forgiveness," "Playing Favorites," and "In an August Mirror"

Prairie Schooner: "All for the Love of You," "Wasps," "Mirage," "Anniversary," and "November Trees"

Shenandoah: "Deep Purple," "Speaking of Belief," "Dumped at Heaven's Gate," and "The Toad"

Southern Quarterly: "Baring the Inevitable"

Southern Review: "The Interview"

Southwest Review: "Knee High"

Spillway: "Taking a Turn with Sappho"

Subtropics: "When did we first"

Valparaiso Poetry Review: "The Visitation"

Western Humanities Review: "First Blood" and "Putting Two and Two Together"

"The Poet" was also published in *Far Out: Poems of the '60s,* ed. Wendy Barker and Dave Parsons, and in *Nasty Women Poets: An Unapologetic Anthology of Subversive Voices,* ed. Grace Bauer and Julie Kane. "The Doll" was published in *The Doll Collection,* ed. Diane Lockward. "Reading Boccaccio" was also published in *A Constellation of Kisses,* ed. Diane Lockward. "Knee High," "At the Gates," and "All for the Love of You" were reprinted on *Vox Populi.* "Case #87 on the Calendar" was reprinted in the *Alabama Literary Review.* "Mirage" was featured on *Poetry Daily.* "Dumped at Heaven's Gate" was selected for inclusion in the *2018 Best of the Net Anthology.*

~~~~~

I am grateful to the *Georgia Review* / Bowers House Writers Retreat and Literary Center and the Lillian E. Smith Center of Piedmont College, where many of these poems were written, and to all the friends and fine writers who have stood by me these many years: Roger Pfingston, Patricia Waters, Roger Mitchell, Jo McDougall, Andrea Hollander, Kim Bridgford, Marianne Boruch, Marilyn Kallet, Dale Kushner, Peggy Shumaker, et al. Special thanks to Wendy Barker and the late Kathryn Stripling Byer for their invaluable help with individual poems and advice in ordering this manuscript. To Bruce, my "sweet young thing," surely a gold crown for his enduring patience and devotion.

"Asking Forgiveness" and "All for the Love of You" are about the death of my mother-in-law, Daisy Gentry, 1919–2013. "All for the love of you" is a line from the song "Daisy Bell (Bicycle Built for Two)," by Harry Dacre, 1892.

"Dumped at Heaven's Gate." The idea for this poem came from my good friend Sean Sexton, a Florida cattle rancher and poet extraordinaire.

The information for "Judith" comes from the biblical account in Judith of the campaign of Holofernes against Judaea.

"Deep Purple" is a song written in 1933 by Peter De Rose, lyrics added five years later by Mitchell Parish.

"Clytemnestra, Unleashed" owes its impetus to Aeschylus's *Agamemnon* from his *Oresteia*.

"Reading Boccaccio." The opening quotation is an Italian saying that Boccaccio uses as the last sentence of the seventh story, second day, in *The Decameron* as translated by G. H. McWilliam.

"Donatello's Prophet." The quotations are from Habakkuk 2:19.

"*Ars Poetica* in a Tilted Chair." The quotation from Flaubert is found in *Flaubert's Parrot*, by Julian Barnes.